Also by Paul Hoyt

Inspirational Works

Surprises on the Road to Enlightenment (2023)

The Levels of Creation (2016)

The Practice of Awakening II: The First Light of Joy –
Over 160 Awakening Lessons and Poems for Your
Transformational Journey (2013)

The Practice of Awakening – 150 Ways to Raise Your
Consciousness Whenever You Choose (2010)

Remember – A Simple, Gentle, Powerful Pathway to Your
Magnificent Potential (2005)

Business Works

Beyond Business Survival – The Key to Thriving in
Business (2013)

The Capital Coaching Program (2010)

The Foundation Factor – Critical Measurements of
Business Strength (2004)

Also by Pas Simpson

Inspirational Works

The Big 365 (2015)

CURING
RACISM

One Conversation,
One Connection,
One Heart at a Time

By Paul Hoyt and Pas Simpson

This book is dedicated to all the children of the world,
for generations to come.

Table of Contents

Pas's Forward

Growing up in Harlem in the 1980s meant there was not much interaction with other cultures. My neighborhood was predominately Black and Latino, and we had a very strong cultural identity.

The Five Percent Nation movement was a very strong influence on me. They were very popular since they called Manhattan "Mecca". They wanted to empower our cultural identity by teaching us that the Black Man was God and the White Man was a grafted devil. They taught us to renounce our teachers and textbooks and to understand that all life began in Africa. They reiterated that all great things started with Black Culture and were then adopted by other people.

My father was a little less extreme than the brothers from the Five Percent that were teaching us in the streets. My father was one of the oldest professors in New York State, and my mother and he preached education as freedom. My father would take my brother and I to the Schomburg Center for Research in Black Culture, which was then the only African American Library in the United States. He would have us spend hours reading and researching facts that were pertinent in shaping our Black identity. He would stress that Black culture did not start in America and did not end with the civil rights movement. He wanted us to know that we were descendants of greatness.

It was different back then because, outside of television, we did not have much interaction with white people. The white people who came into our neighborhood were either teachers or drug abusers and we could tell the difference by the time of day they came into the neighborhood. The teachers would be long gone by five PM, would not be there during the summers, and were always nervous around large crowds. The drug abusers normally entered the neighborhood around 6 PM, were very bold around large crowds to get their fix and were there year-round.

These images skewed my view of white people. I saw them as authoritarians or drug abusers. This perception did not change when I attended prep school. I was one of two black students on campus and experienced quite a culture shock my first year. It felt horrible because I felt like I didn't belong unless I was doing something athletically. The other students were wealthy white children with money to spare, and many of them wasted it on alcohol and drugs, reinforcing the stereotype I already had in my mind. I still remember someone asking me if I could get them some ecstasy. At that time, I had no idea what it was, but I knew I could call someone back home to find it. That transaction just made my beliefs even stronger. It was not until the summer I spent with Patti Ota that everything changed.

Patti was one of the warmest people I ever met. She let me stay in her home so I could compete in summer league with my basketball team. She stressed the importance of education, but was gentle in her approach and not as harsh in her delivery as my mother. She was extra loving to her children and she now considered me one of them. She did not allow drinking or drugs in her home, so my stereotype was being challenged. She was stern, yet gave us a lot of freedom to make good decisions. Patti was not the white

2

devil I had been taught about nor was she a drug abuser. Could there be more to learn about white people than I thought?

My interaction with Patti and her two sons Kenji and Miki opened my eyes to a whole new world. Kenji and I competed against each other in sports, but I was a natural athlete with a real competitive spirit, and Miki was the younger brother that was always so impressed. Patti became a mother figure in my life and was very influential in my decision to go to Lehigh University, where she worked in the President's office.

After the birth of my first son, Patti stepped in like a loving grandmother. She made sure he had everything he needed and that I did not let his birth become a distraction from me graduating from college. Even during my real black nationalist days, Patti understood my views and I would still call her mom. She was so good to me and my family, my mother encouraged me to call her mom. Almost twenty-five years after I spent the summer at her home, I can say she changed my perception on race and life, and I am still proud to call her my second mom.

Paul's Forward

When I was growing up in Kansas in the 1950s there was not much interaction with other cultures. My neighborhood was completely white, as was my elementary school. I am told that there were a few black kids in my junior high school, but I don't remember them.

There were no organizations that I knew of that taught that whites were superior, it was just more or less an unspoken assumption. We learned about George Washington Carver and a few other famous black men, but they were presented as exceptions.

I lived in a completely segregated world until high school. Then, a predominantly black middle school fed into the same high school as my junior high school did. We came to see blacks as great athletes, and I was always amazed at their prowess in football, basketball, and track. Golf, tennis, cross country, swimming, and wrestling were almost completely white. I can't remember having any black kids in any of my classes.

Outside of school, I had practically no interaction with black people. They never came into our neighborhoods, so we only saw them in school and at school events.

This early experience skewed my view of black people. I saw them as challenged in school, but gifted in athletics. I didn't have much interaction with them at all, even through college. I remember Martin Luther King and the civil rights events of the 60's, but they didn't have much impact on white bread Wichita Kansas.

That all changed one day in the late 70's. My sister Linda had married a Brazilian man with dark skin, and their children also had darker skin that my other family members. Their eldest girl, Kayce, had married a black man, and they had six boys in short order.

When I went to visit them in Houston Texas, those boys were very excited to see their uncle Paul, having heard a lot of good things about me. They wanted to play ball, work puzzles, and play games on the computer. They were eager to show me their toys and share them with me. They wanted to play! I was surprised and taken aback. They had accepted me with open arms. They were totally color blind, and I was not.

And then Kayce handed me her youngest son Mason, an infant only a few months old. As I held him in my arms, my heart melted. I saw him as the precious child that he was and loved him immediately, just as I did when I held my own sons in my arms for the first time. My view of darker-skinned people changed forever.

I realized in that moment how prejudiced and wrong I had been. It was quite the unexpected awakening.

Introduction

What do a little old white guy from Kansas and a black dude from Harlem have in common?

Everything.

We both love our families. We both appreciate and respect each other. We are both learning and growing. And we both have a sense of urgency about doing everything we can to reduce the impact of racism and minimize the incredible tragedies that racial prejudice and discrimination cause in the world.

Young men and women are shot and killed every day due to racism. Dreams are crushed and incredible potential is suppressed and left unrealized. A very large segment of our population lives in a frightening and challenging culture due to the enduring impact of slavery. Children are dying, and mothers and fathers are left crying.

Racism is the belief that characteristics and abilities can be attributed to people simply because of their ethnic heritage, and that some racial groups are superior to others. Racial prejudice and discrimination have been used as powerful weapons encouraging fear or hatred of others in times of conflict and war, and even during economic downturns.

As it turns out, racism is primarily used to obtain an economic advantage. It is a tool of frightened, greedy, and cruel people. It is not the tool of conscious, compassionate, intelligent people.

We believe that racism is an indication of a lack of education and experience. It is one of those unintelligent beliefs passed down from generation to generation, such as "the earth is flat" or "the sun revolves around the earth".

We believe that a conscious and intelligent conversation about the history and the impact of racism will help eliminate it, much like a science course in astronomy reduces the number of people who believe that our planet is flat and is the center of the universe.

We believe that it is time to Cure Racism.

This is not a religious book or a book that is loosely put together. This is a book that will be able to provide a true understanding, dispel some myths, and erase the misconceptions many of us have been taught to accept.

This is a courageous journey of two men raised with different cultural backgrounds and different skin colors, but with one common understanding: that we are all brothers and sisters, that our differences in skin color, language, and dress are just superficial and quite meaningless.

It is important that we see past the lies that have been previously accepted by many cultures if the human race is to flourish at its highest capacity. Dividing humanity by language, color, or culture only hurts us all.

Most importantly, it is clear to us that advances in technology are coming much quicker than increases in emotional intelligence. Our ability to kill each other is greatly outpacing our ability to get along, and we have to do everything we can to keep tribal conflicts from destroying us all.

The solution is simple: when we learn to see through the superficial differences that divide us, we will be able to discover the common values that unite us.

Note: This book is intentionally very short. While very large books have been written on the subjects of each of the chapters, we believe the impact and the message is best delivered concisely and powerfully. We encourage you to read it in one sitting, and then again after a few days.

Then, take inspired action to do what you can do to help all of us cure the dreaded disease of racism.

Chapter 1: The Origins of Racism

Ulu woke up tired, hungry, and in a lot of pain. She had given birth a few days earlier and was happy that she and her baby had survived. Many new mothers and tiny babies did not. She was grateful for the care given to her by her sisters and the other women in the tribe. She knew that neither her nor her baby would have survived without them. Her sisters cleaned her up and brought her food and water. The other young mothers shared their milk with her baby, as hers was yet to come in. And the men of the village brought them skins and furs, built their shelters, and protected them all. Life was tough in 10,000 B.C.

We human beings are fantastic creatures: we care for each other; we nurture our children and each other; we are capable of incredible artistry in music, dance, poetry, and painting; we produce phenomenal physical and mental accomplishments; and we are growing as a society in emotional intelligence and stability. We are becoming more civilized over time.

But unfortunately, we have a darker side: We can be temperamental, violent, judgmental, abusive, and we have a long way to go in our journey toward great wisdom and unconditional love. And racism is far too often the source of, or a contributing factor in our violence.

Racism comes from three things: our tribal instinct, our herd mentality, and the fact that we humans are born fighters and pack hunters.

Our Tribal Instinct

As it turns out, human beings are poorly equipped to survive on the earth: we have no fangs or claws, we are comparatively small, we have no armor, and we are quite slow. In contrast, a tiger can weigh 890 pounds and run 40 miles an hour in short bursts. We are born helpless, as our brains are very immature. Babies can't reach full size and fit through a woman's pelvis. It would take another 9-12 months in a mother's womb for a human being to have the natural adaptive quality that a chimpanzee does when they are born. A human mother simple cannot supply herself and her baby with the nutrition required for her baby to mature. Others must provide sources of nutrition and protection from the elements.

And just as it takes a family for mothers and babies to survive, it takes a tribe for families to survive. There is strength and safety in numbers. To protect our families and to hunt effectively, we organized into tribes. In fact, the commitment to the tribe was the only way for our species to survive. In his book *The Human Baby,* James Kimmel notes, "Humans evolved in the natural world and evolved to adapt to that world. Crucial to our success as a species when we lived in that world was our capacity to collaborate as a unified group. When we lived in small groups as hunter-gatherers… our strength was in our ability for combined and unified functioning, not in our individual and separate skills, powers, possessions, or wealth."

It was our groups - the families and the tribes - that enabled our survival and evolution. And most of the ones who didn't have an appreciation and respect for the family and tribe were cast out. The tribe simply didn't have the resources to care for people who could not in some way pull their own weight. We have been genetically conditioned to identify with our tribe, and we tend to not see ourselves as members of any other groups, especially those groups who are not in some way supporting our families and tribe.

And **that's at the core of the racism problem: the tendency to see ourselves in groups.** We have an "us" and "them" mentality, which psychologists call the "in group" and the "out group" mentality. We seem to relish the division; we want to identify with a few instead of identifying with all. We divide ourselves along political lines, religious lines, lifestyle lines, and around racial boundaries. It is our tribal instinct.

Our Herd Mentality

Sam was scared - really scared. The evening started innocently enough, hanging out with the guys, having some drinks and talking trash. Then Joe, the biggest and meanest one, got all fired up to "go get some money". Then someone brought out a gun, and before he knew it, he was in the car pulling up to the liquor store and shit was about to go down. He couldn't just get out and run away - he would be seen as weak, and he knew what would happen then. So he gulped, pretended to be tough, and silently prayed.

As our tribal instincts evolved, we developed a herd mentality. We learned to follow the leader, often ingratiating

13

ourselves to the leader. We became addicted to approval and needed desperately to belong to our groups. We found it very difficult to go against the crowd and against authority, especially when the leaders discouraged, suppressed, and punished that dissension. Peer pressure can be an incredibly powerful force.

In his article entitled "Chimps Are Less Susceptible to Peer Pressure than Humans," Adam Benton notes, "Humans are very susceptible to peer pressure and the watchful eyes of others. This vulnerability to peer pressure is so strong that even cartoons of eyes watching us can make us less likely to cheat. In fact, images of eyes reduce the level of cheating even more than a strongly worded sign saying 'Don't Cheat'.

In short, those who behaved correctly when being watched by other members of their group flourished as they weren't being thrown out of groups for being a possible danger to the group. This trait spread throughout the population through natural selection until we all had an innate, subconscious response to seeing eyes, even if they were cartoon eyes, that makes us more likely to follow the rules." Even these cartoon eyes can trigger feelings of our addictions to approval and our need for belonging, and that need caused us to develope a real "us and them" mentality.

In a 2013 study, Englemann, Herman, and Omasello discovered that with children, just a difference in clothing triggered changes. If the observer was wearing the same color as the person who was asked to donate to another child, then they were much more generous, giving twice as many stickers to the unknown child.

In a 2014 study, researchers at the University of Washington, babies 15 months old were seen to have already developed a preference for playing with an experimenter who looked like them, even when another had given them more toys. They felt safer, or at least, wanted to support ones they perceived as being in their "group".

(see http://www.telegraph.co.uk/news/science/science-news/10770563/Babies-show-racial-bias-study-finds.html)

We developed a herd behavior and we became more emotional in tribal settings, such that our IQ is actually reduced when we are with the tribe. And our mob mentality is still alive, even during celebrations of victory. We have all seen pictures on TV of celebrations gone awry when people start setting fires and turning over cars, even if their team has just won a major sports championship.

We also have a tendency when we gather in tribes to dehumanize members of other tribes. In his book *Less than Human,* David Livingston Smith notes that in ancient Chinese, Egyptian, and Mesopotamian literature, there are repeated references to enemies as subhuman creatures. The Nazis referred to the Jews as rats. In Rwanda, the Hutus referred to the Tutsis as cockroaches, which therefore made it a lot easier for them to enact genocide against the people who they did not see as being human in the same way that they saw members of their own tribe.

So we need a tribe to survive, we naturally divide into tribes, we have a herd mentality, and we are heavily influenced by peer pressure. Over time, we developed a real "us and them" mentality. That would be interesting enough, but unfortunately it can become tragic because we are also born fighters.

Born Fighters

Our species became hunters, killers, and protectors in order to survive. We became warriors, and we used all our cleverness to create tools and tactics of war. There is evidence of this across many cultures and throughout history. In the book *Constant Battles: The Myth of the Peaceful, Noble Savage,* the authors LeBlanc and Register note that peaceful societies are an exception. About 90-95% of known societies engage in war. The attrition rate of numerous close-quarter clashes, which characterize warfare in tribal warrior society, produced casualty rates of up to 60%. That's in stark contrast to modern warfare, which produces casualty rates of only about 1%. There is strong evidence in brutal warring behavior across all continents. It wasn't that the Europeans brought their brutal behaviors to the Americas; there is evidence that the indigenous peoples of America also engaged in brutal warfare. It's true in Africa, South America, and all other continents. It is inherent to the species; it's not just any one tribe that was that way.

We even loved our battles so much that we created fighting games. There is an ancient Greek game called pankration, which was like today's mixed martial arts, except the only action they didn't allow was biting or gouging the eyes—everything else was okay. They kept fighting until people either died or gave up completely. In ancient Egypt, they had a fisherman's joust, which was an Egyptian blood sport where men were sent out in boats and whacked at each other with paddles or spiked objects until one of the parties fell into the water bloodied and was eaten by crocodiles. In the Roman coliseum, we had wild animal murders of innocent people. In the ancient times, we had the Viking skin-pulling contest, which was tug-of-war with fire in the middle, so the losing tribe actually got drug through the fire. Perhaps the worst of all was the ulama, a Mayan sport similar to basketball, except they used hips, and instead of the ball, they used a human head. We suspect the way they got these heads was from losers of previous contests. Even today, we have football, wrestling, boxing, and a terribly savage sport called mixed martial arts. Our violent, cruel, punishing nature has been a persistent problem through the ages.

So we are a highly intelligent, emotional species, driven by our survival instinct, our need to procreate, our tribal instinct, our herd mentality, our "us and them" mentality, and our fighting, warring nature. It is genetic and natural for us to group together and to fight other groups.

In his article "The Tribal Instinct Hypothesis," Mark Van Vugt says, "If a team of alien biologists were to collect data about different life forms on Planet Earth, what observations would they make about us humans? They would witness the cities, churches, schools, and hospitals that we built and note that we are very good at helping fellow humans in sometimes very large groups. But they would also see evidence of our darker side: All around the world, they would witness incidents of violence and warfare between armies, militias, religious groups, and street gangs. Upon their return, the alien research team would likely conclude that humans are a tribal species, capable of both extreme benevolence toward members of ingroups and extreme hostility toward members of outgroups."

Pre-Workshop Activities

1. Take a few minutes and imagine what it would be like to be a young mother giving birth in a remote village with no electricity, medicine, or health care of any kind. Imagine how painful and frightening it would be, and how totally dependent you would be on your family and your tribe to survive.

2. Imagine trying to protect your family from a bear or other large predator. If all you had were rocks and sticks, how many people would you need to have in a hunting party? What if you had a bow and arrow or a spear?

Chapter 2: Evolution in Isolation

Atah was as excited as she could be. Her five sons had left home decades ago to seek their fame and fortune in far off lands, and they were all coming home to see her one last time before she passed. They had not seen her or each other at all since they left.

When her sons arrived, they were all quite different. One had spent a lot of time in the sun, and his skin was quite dark. Another had eaten foods for 20 years that had turned his skin sallow, and yet another spent his time in colder climates, and was quite pale. They each wore different clothes and spoke with a different accent. They preferred different foods. They worshiped different gods. One had been told that he should never cut his hair as a sign of his faith, and another was completely shaven and bald as a sign of his devotion to God.

They were so amazingly different that it was very difficult for her to see and remember that they once looked and talked quite the same.

But Atah loved them all, as much as she ever did. She was amazed and delighted by their differences. She gained great wisdom about the impact of their environments and their culture and saw first-hand what evolution in isolation can do.

And so it is with the human race. Tribes migrated away from Africa more than 100,000 years ago and evolved in relative isolation. They developed different languages, religions, and cultures.

But we all have the same mothers and fathers. We are all distant brothers and sisters, and we are now having a global reunion enabled by advances in transportation and the power of technology.

There is only one race, the human race. Whether we are short, tall, skinny, fat, speak a foreign language or have a different hue in our pigmentation, we are all the same race.

Many people have been fooled over the years into thinking that the language they speak, the color of their skin, and the culture that they represent are all a part of their race. That is a falsehood. If you speak a different language, that does not change your race. If you represent a different culture, that does not change your race. If your skin color has a darker hue to it, that does not change your race.

There are people who have the same color of their complexion who all have different cultures that they represent. If they grew up in South America or Africa or even Europe, they would have different cultural elements than we do. Even if they grew up in the same country but in different regions, like if they grew up in the South or the West in the United States, the way they carry themselves in this culture will be different. Color, culture, and language do not change your race. We are all products of our environment.

Pre-Workshop Activities

1. Think about how your family members changed when they moved away for a few years. Did they wear the same clothes and eat the same foods, or did they pick up some of the customs local to their new location?

2. Imagine going to live on another continent for a thousand years. What changes would you expect?

Chapter 3: The History of Slavery Around the World

Ekat was angry, tired, and very frightened. The enemy had come in the middle of the night and literally stolen him and his family from their village. They were dragged away in shackles and beaten. They had little to eat or drink, and now they were being forced into the hold of a big boat, to be taken God knows where. He wondered what would become of them. He wondered whether his children, or his children's children would ever taste freedom again. He was determined to do anything he had to do to survive, including bowing at the feet of the kidnappers and abusers. But secretly, when the masters were not around, he taught his children the truth of their journey and prayed that they would someday be free.

Slavery was unheard of back when the human race consisted of tribes of hunter-gatherers and primitive farmers. The tribes grew and hunted for their own food and had no use for slaves. There were tribal wars to be sure, but capturing and managing slaves only came about with "civilization".

As people gathered in towns and villages, there became an economic reason for cheap labor – and that was to grow, harvest, and move food from the country to the village, and to build and maintain the village infrastructure. Large farms and large workshops needed cheap labor that would benefit the owners. With industry and technology, it became feasible to control and use a slave population.

Slavery can be traced back to the earliest of all written records. When one tribe conquered another, they killed the men and took the women and children as slaves. It was a common practice in almost every ancient civilization, including Ancient Egypt, Ancient China, the Akkadian Empire, Assyria, Ancient Greece, the Roman Empire, the Islamic Caliphate and Sultanate, and the pre-Columbian civilizations of the Americas.

Wars became the major suppliers of slaves since they were frequent. Those who lost a war were captured, became slaves of the conquering group, and became their workers. They were allowed to live in return for providing labor.

There were other sources of slaves. Pirates offered their captives for sale, criminals could be sentenced to slavery, and the impoverished would sell their children into slavery. Slavery was used as a punishment for debt and crimes, and often became the fate of abandoned and orphaned children. Slaves would have children, and those children would also be slaves. Slaves were considered part of the valuable possessions of the slave owner, much like buildings and farm animals, and were traded, bought, and sold much in the same manner.

Slavery has had many variations throughout history, including serfdom and other classes of the population. While the serf typically had some rights, he or she was bound to the land or to the lord and was not free to move about or choose locations or occupations.

During the 7th Century BC in Greece, both Sparta and Athens depended on forced labor. In Sparta, they described it as serfdom. Helots of Sparta lived in their hereditary land and were believed to be conquered hence they worked forcefully in their Spartan masters' lands. They, however, retained their rights. In Athens, slaves lacked conventional rights though their working conditions varied depending on where they worked. Most Athenians were domestic slaves; the male slaves were more of stewards and personal assistants who took care of the household property, while the females cared for their masters' children.

In Rome, slavery was widely practiced and with much cruelty. Those that worked in the mines were whipped frequently. They worked in chains in the fields and were forced to fight as gladiators in public arenas, often to the death. There were many slave uprisings during the Roman Empire, the most famous of which led by Spartacus.

After the end of the Roman Empire, slavery continued in the Medieval Ages around the Mediterranean and Europe. Vikings and other nations also kept slaves. Towns such as Dublin, Rome, and London had slave markets. In the 10th century, the Germans expanded eastward resulting to the capture of many Slavs (the racial generic name for slave). During the same period, there was delivery of slaves to the Black Sea Region of Russia.

Slavery wasn't unique to Europe. In Central America, there was also slavery long before the Europeans arrived. Mayans and Aztecs made slaves do all the difficult work. Most of them were captured in wars, but people would also sell themselves and their children when in extreme poverty.

Slavery continued to the South of the Mediterranean with dynasties of Arabs taking slaves from Africa, where slavery was commonplace. Zawila, in the Sahara desert, was a famous trading station for slaves. Slaves were captured around Lake Chad and sold to Arabs, and the practice later spread from Spain to Persia. By the 7th century, slavery was accepted as a normal way of life in Arabia in the era of Muhammad.

The Portuguese were the first commercial slave traders, starting in 1418. Their expeditions into the Sub-Saharan region of Africa and West Africa opened up another channel for the transportation of slaves. After gaining an economic advantage and guarantee of their prosperity, they monopolized slave trade in Guinea. This wasn't a new thing in Africa, as Africans had sold their fellow Africans to Arabs for many years, but the Portuguese made the market bigger. Current estimates are that about 12 million Africans were shipped across the Atlantic, and the total number purchased by the traders was considerably higher. Cape Verde plantations used slave labor to grow cotton and indigo. Other slaves were used to weave and dye in the factories to create cloth. Most slaves were sold to West Indies and Brazil while others went to North America and British colonies.

By the 18th-century, slave trade had evolved into a practice known as the Triangular Trade. British ships took manufactured goods to Africa, exchanged them for slaves, took the slaves to West Indies, and then took back molasses from sugarcane to Britain, which was transformed to rum. The conditions to which the African slaves were subjected were quite cruel. Most of them died of diseases in the ships that transported them. Others were forced to work in plantations and were often separated from their families after arrival in the West Indies. Those who survived lived in small huts that had a bed, a bench, a few utensils, and very little else.

Additionally, there were European slaves in North Africa who were captured by pirates as they sailed the Mediterranean. Pirates from North Africa also raided the coastal regions of Ireland, Spain, Portugal, Italy, France, and Southwest England for slaves. They also went to extreme areas such as Iceland and captured their inhabitants. White slave trade ended in 1830 after the region was conquered by the French.

In the 18th century, the European opinion of slavery changed, and many came out against slavery. Quakers were the first people to act after deciding to drive out any members who were involved in any activities that led to slave trade. A Society for the Abolition of the Slave Trade was formed. In the end of the 18th century, there was the presentation of petitions to parliament to end slave trade. Denmark ended slave trade first in 1792, followed by Britain in 1807. Other European countries followed, with Brazil ending the slave trade in 1851 and the United States in 1865. Abolishment continued in the 19th century in China and Morocco, Afghanistan, Iran, Saudi Arabia; Mauritania was the last country to outlaw slavery, in 1981.

One of the most recent and tragic occurrences of slavery came in World War II, when the Germans captured and enslaved millions of Jews. Some were executed immediately, some were the victims of torturous experiments, and others were simply worked to death.

As a world, we are not that far removed from the days of a conquering tribe enslaving and dealing harshly with those who were conquered. And there are still slaves today, although the term "human trafficking" is often used to soften the conversation. EndSlaveryNow.org estimates that there are between 21 million and 45 million people trapped in some form of slavery today (as of May, 2020), the worst incidences of which are forced marriages and sex trafficking.

Pre-Workshop Activities

1. Take a few minutes and imagine what it would be like to be a slave. What would you miss about freedom? What would you tell your children?

Chapter 4: The History of Slavery in the U.S.

The mothers' screams were terrifying. As Sarah stood in line with her family, she was in shock at what she feared was about to happen. Her husband and children were all up for sale, and the odds of them all being purchased by the same master were not good. The families that went before were repeatedly separated. Husbands and wives would probably never see their children again, and perhaps they would be separated, too. She held her children close as their time on the block approached, fearing all too much that the next screams would be hers.

Slavery in the United States began in 1619, when the first slaves were brought to Jamestown, Virginia. A Dutch ship, called the White Lion, captured 20 enslaved Africans, and then traded the slaves for food and supplies to the colonials. After that, slavery grew in the Americas during the great migration of 1618-1623 from about 450 to 4,000 people. This was also when the mortality rates were extremely high due to diseases, warfare with the Indians, and malnutrition.

The majority of the slaves in the United States were healthy and able-bodied Africans. Others were Irish, Germans, Scottish, and English who were brought in from Europe having debts for passage over the sea. Some were indentured servants, in essence, temporary slaves. This was the first generation of Africans who were allowed their freedom after a couple of years. However, in 1664 in Maryland, it was declared that all Africans in the colony would serve as slaves for life. Slavery was initially not inflicted exclusively on Africans. In South Carolina, for example, Native Americans were captured and sold to the West Indies.

At the end of the 17th Century, African slaves grew to larger populations. Labor at Chesapeake tobacco was mainly supplied by the white indentured servants. The transition from servants to slaves then rose with the scarcity of servants, the demand for Chesapeake tobacco, the improved life expectancy among African Americans and the enhancement of their value as slaves for life. Slaves became more useful on large farms with cash crops that required lots of labor, such as tobacco and cotton. However, after the American Revolution, most colonists, especially in the North, likened the oppression they faced from the British to the oppression of the black slaves, and called for the abolishment of slavery. Slavery had proven unprofitable and was beginning to lose popularity in the North, primarily because of the expense of housing slaves during cold winter months and the lack of large farms.

Slavery become more popular in the South after Northerner Eli Whitney invented the cotton gin in 1793, which made it easier to remove seeds from raw cotton fibers. Cotton was easily grown in the South and so a large market developed. Ginned cotton became the raw material for the textile industry in England. With the device gaining popularity, there was a transition from the tobacco production to a large-scale production in cotton, which brought with it the dependence of slave labor. While slavery did not spread in the North, many businesspeople profited from slave trade and investments in the cotton plantations. Later on, slavery was done away with in the North, but the 'peculiar institution' remained important to the South. In spite of the efforts made by the Congress to outlaw African Slave Trade in 1808, the slave population tripled with the boom of domestic trade.

Southerners were caught in a dilemma between the benefits that slavery brought in and the moral and constitutional issues of the institution. They decided to be more defensive of slavery and advocated for it. They gave excuses and arguments that African children could not take good care of themselves, therefore, slavery was the generous institution that kept the children busy, dressed, and fed. Northerners who refused slavery did not believe in its benevolence, but they agreed on the inferiority nature of blacks as compared to the white population.

The anti-slavery movement gradually gained power. Individual abolitionists such as publisher and editor William Lloyd voiced their concerns on the issue and became increasingly violent. There were others who had escaped slavery and were educated, especially Fredrick Douglas, who wrote heartfelt attacks of the institution. Harriet Beecher Stowe's *Uncle Tom's Cabin* novel in 1852 helped fuel the abolitionist cause. There was also the Harriet Tubman Underground Railroad that secretly helped slaves escape to freedom in the Northern states.

Despite the owners' claims, the reality was that slaves received dehumanizing treatment. A family of slaves was often sold to different owners, thus separating them, and whipping was the preferred method of punishment method. To top it off, in 1857, The US Supreme Court in the Dred Scott decision ruled against the slaves, declaring that they were a subhuman property with no citizenship rights. This denied them the right to protest any mistreatments. Out of fear of open rebellion, Southern slaves would fake illnesses, sabotage farm equipment, organize slowdowns, commit arson, or even murder at times, and run away whenever they could.

At the time of the civil war, the slave population in the United States stood at four million. 95% of blacks lived in the South, comprising one third of the population there as opposed to 1% of the population of the North. The central issue in politics in the 1850s involved rich Southern slave owners moving into the western territories, bringing their slaves, and buying the best lands to the detriment of the average white farmers. The abolition of slavery, then, was as economically motivated as it was a moral cause.

The Whig Party split and collapsed on the slavery issue and was replaced in the North by the new Republican Party, which was dedicated to stopping the expansion of slavery. Republicans gained a majority in every Northern state by absorbing a faction of anti-slavery Democrats, and the warning that slavery was a backward system that undercut democracy and economic modernization. Numerous compromise proposals were put forward, but they all collapsed.

The Civil War that followed changed the Nation's future. The election of Abraham Lincoln as president prompted the secession of seven Southern states within three months. Four more followed, and then the civil war broke out in 1861 to 1865. Its aim was to preserve the American nation, but it would later lead to abolishing slavery. The growing anti-slavery sentiments, military necessities, and self-emancipation of the Africans who fled enslavement in the South to become Union troops made it an abolition war, too. After the Union victory at Antietam in 1862, Lincoln proclaimed the Preliminary Emancipation Proclamation. In the beginning of 1863, slaves were declared free and as members of the state.

Many lives were lost in the war, and a multitude of challenges were experienced during the reconstruction period. Former slaves who had survived their ordeals and the war received citizenship rights and the same protection as the whites under the constitution.

But despite the abolition of slave trade, constitutional provisions were ignored, and former slaves found it difficult to get a grip on the postwar economy because of the regressive contracts such as sharecropping and the restrictive black codes. The resentment towards the North by Southerners was then directed to the former slaves, whom they blamed for the economic misfortune of the South.

Pre-Workshop Activities

1. Were any of your ancestors slave owners? What if they had been? What would you say to them today?

2. Could you justify owning another person - and her children? How so?

Chapter 5: A Century of Oppression and Slow Progress

Miles was so excited! He was going with his dad to see the Dodgers play baseball, and Jackie Robinson was playing! Miles loved baseball and even dreamed of playing pro some day. Jackie had paved the way, so now he knew it was possible. While Jackie didn't hit any home runs that day, he played pretty good. But on the way out, his joy was short-lived. He heard a couple of white guys cursing Jackie and calling him names, saying that those niggers should never be allowed on the field. He followed his dad's lead. He looked down at the ground, kept quiet, and slowly walked away.

After the African Americans had gained their emancipation from slavery, they faced near total discrimination in all aspects of their lives. With no resources and little education, they struggled from the start to establish any semblance of financial stability. And most of the white population was not inspired to help them.

Segregation and unequal distribution of resources were especially felt in the Southern states where most African Americans lived. There was great promise in the 14th amendment of 1868, which declared protection of the laws to all citizens, but in practice, local governments passed Jim Crow laws, which made segregation and prejudice 'legal' and even mandatory.

African Americans were forced to have separate schools, theaters, bathrooms, drinking fountains, buses, trains, and restaurants from those that were used by whites. While many of the laws called for "separate but equal", that was almost never the case. Blacks were at higher risk of being victimized by the mob rule, lynching, and horrific violence. Segregation and the unequal distribution of resources were especially felt in the Southern states, where most African Americans lived.

The conditions in which they lived were unpleasant, to say the least. They had to endure substandard and inadequate facilities, were not able to exercise their right to vote, and were referred to in dehumanizing terms such as 'nigger' and 'coon'. Almost all of their public services were underfunded when compared to the funding for white public services.

While blacks were often successful running for local offices, their votes were often suppressed for state and national elections. Voter registration requirements were specifically designed to make it difficult or impossible for blacks to be fairly represented. Poll taxes, literacy tests, and proof of residency were just some of the tactics used. In many states, the white majority did everything they could to make the blacks politically invisible. In some states, white voters registered before the Emancipation Proclamation were grandfathered in and didn't have to pass those same literacy or competency tests.

The Ku Klux Klan

The Ku Klux Klan (or KKK), a right-wing hate group and terrorist organization, flourished after the Civil War. It began in Tennessee sometime around 1865 – 1866 by former officers of the confederate army. While it began as just a fraternal organization, members quickly began to focus on committing violence against freedmen and those who supported them.

From 1868 to 1871, the KKK was suspected in more than 400 lynchings. They were largely broken up then, but reformed after the release of the movie "The Birth of a Nation" in 1915, which glorified the actions of the early years of the Klan. In 1920, the KKK claimed to have millions of members, but was believed to only have 30,000 members by 1930.

The KKK saw another resurgence after 1950. It continues even today as a secret society, with thousands of members. In response to massive immigration of people from southern and eastern Europe, the Klan had an anti-immigrant, anti-Catholic and anti-Jewish stance, in addition to exercising oppression of blacks.

Segregation in the Military

The United States Military was no different from the rest of the country, with mandatory segregation until 1948. Blacks began to serve in both the Army and the Navy in the Civil War, and in 1866, the Buffalo Soldiers were established by Congress, but they were rarely used in combat. That changed towards the end of World War II because of a shortage of troops. Buffalo Soldiers were offered the opportunity to volunteer for combat, and they served admirably. The Buffalo Soldiers were finally disbanded and the services totally integrated in late 1951.

Segregation in Sports

As is often the case, athletics provided an opening for the lessening of segregation. In the 1936 Olympics, Jesse Owens won the 100-meter dash, John Woodruff won the 800-meter dash, Cornelius Johnson won the high jump, and 15 other blacks were a part of the US track and field team. But they came home to a land still steeped in discrimination and segregation. Mack Robinson, Jackie Robinson's older brother, won the silver medal in the 100-meter dash, and came home to work as a street sweeper. None of those Olympians were invited to the White House. None shook the president's hand, as did so many of their fellow Olympians.

In baseball, blacks were prohibited from playing until 1946. Blacks formed their own Negro leagues until Jackie Robinson was signed by the Los Angeles Dodgers. Larry Doby followed the next year. The breakthrough came when the new baseball commissioner, Happy Chandler, reasoned that he simply could not in good conscience forbid blacks from playing professional baseball when so many had fought so valiantly alongside whites in World War II.

By the late 1950's, blacks were as common in professional baseball as they were in the rest of the population.

Curiously, the Boston Red Sox held out, and were the last team to be integrated in 1959. They changed their policy largely because they had failed to make the playoffs for 20 years in a row by refusing to take advantage of black talent.

Professional football didn't have a much better record, with a few black players popping up every so often until 1934, at which time an informal agreement among team owners put an end to that. No black players were present from then until after World War II. The ice was broken in 1946 when the Los Angeles Coliseum required that the Rams have a least one black player before they would rent the stadium to them. That was the same year that Jackie Robinson first started playing for the Los Angeles Dodgers. Black players slowly began to appear, and by 1952, every team except the Washington Redskins had at least one black player. The Redskins held out until 1962.

The American Football league was far more tolerant, and when they merged with the National Football League in 1970, discrimination was largely over.

As late as 1960, there was segregated seating in professional arenas. Jeppensen Stadium, where the Houston Oilers played, required that blacks be seated only in the end zones, even if the rest of the stadium was virtually empty. They finally reversed the policy in 1965 in order to host an all-pro game. Tulane stadium in New Orleans was also integrated for the Sugar Bowl in 1965.

The Great Migration

Between 1916 and 1970, six million African Americans moved out of the rural South to cities in the Northeast, Midwest, and West. In 1910, more than 90 percent of the African American population lived in the American South, and only 20% lived in cities. When the Great Migration was over, only 53 percent of the African American population remained in the South, and more than 80% lived in cities.

This was one of the greatest migrations in history. And it meant that black families lost much of their social and economic base, leaving behind what they knew to find a better life with less discrimination. The stress of the upheaval contributed greatly to the social disruption in the black population.

Interracial Marriage and the Black Codes

Interracial marriage was outlawed in the seven states in the lower South in 1865 and 1866 with the passing of the Black Codes, which severely limited freedoms. Interracial marriage was also outlawed in some Northern states, including Indiana, Illinois, and Michigan. The codes also compelled them to work as laborers for low wages and restricted their movements. In many cases, it was legal for governments to arrest freedmen on vagrancy charges and commit them to involuntary labor. In some cases, black men were considered vagrants if they were not working in a job managed by a white man. They were also often used in convict leasing systems, which was another form of slavery. Convict leasing systems were so popular that many states didn't have an established prison system until late in the 19th century.

Southern state legislatures continued to pass laws restricting the rights and freedoms of blacks until the civil rights movement of the 1950s and 1960s. Some of the vagrancy laws remained on the books until 1972.

Interracial marriage was not fully legalized in the US until 1967. In many states, interracial sexual relations were also illegal.

Pre-Workshop Activities

1. Talk to someone who was around in the 1950's or before and ask them about segregation. If you can, ask someone who is descended from slaves.

2. Imagine if our country was still segregated. What changes in the infrastructure would need to be in place? How expensive would that be?

Chapter 6: Civil Rights in the U.S.

All of a sudden, the cops were right there! And they were arresting her! I was sitting right there in the back of the bus with the other blacks, just like we were supposed to, minding our own business. And then this white troublemaker demanded that this black woman in the seat across the aisle from me give up her seat so he could plop his white ass down where it didn't belong. She refused - she could have called him a lot of names, but she was mostly silent - and within minutes the cops came and took her away. And I rode with him and his smug expression for 6 more blocks before I finally just got out and walked the rest of the way home. I'm so pissed off. I'm never going to ride a bus again until this is set right!

Harry Truman, president from 1945 to 1953, had long held onto his racist attitudes, but in 1948, he ordered the end of discrimination in the civil service and the armed forces. He realized that it damaged the United States' reputation. This helped bring the civil rights issue for the African Americans to national attention. This was also when African American soldiers who had fought in the liberation of Europe felt the need to fight discrimination and liberate themselves when they came back home. A huge step forward came with the *Brown v. Board of Education* decision of 1954 when the Supreme Court struck down the "separate but equal" doctrine that had been the basis of discrimination since 1868, nearly 100 years earlier.

A year later, in 1955, there were three shocking incidents that stirred up both activists and the ordinary folks who were fed up with the injustices. In Mississippi, Emmet Till, a 14-year-old African American teenager, was murdered. This was after allegations were made that he had flirted with a white girl. His body had been badly mutilated, and all who saw the pictures found them to be revolting. A few months later, Rosa Parks was arrested for not giving up her seat in the colored section of a bus to a white passenger when the white section was full. The Montgomery Bus Boycott that followed brought increased awareness of the power that came with civil disobedience and non-violent protests. And in 1956, the court ruled on the desegregation of buses, but unfortunately, they could not eliminate all of the violence. Many people risked their lives for freedom and equality.

The activists were gaining momentum and with the successful desegregation of buses and schools, then President Eisenhower realized the importance of gaining support from the African American voters. In 1957 he initiated the Civil Rights Act, which was the first action by congress in 82 years. The law banned discrimination, making it illegal, and provided the legal authority to prosecute anyone who violated the law. At that time, approximately 20% of the African Americans had registered as voters, and they were now able to begin registering in much greater numbers. However, there were very weak sanctions against anyone who prevented them from voting. Violence and bombings against the African Americans in churches and schools increased and resulted in a new Civil Rights bill in 1960 that had with it penalties for those that violated court orders.

Dr. Martin Luther King Jr. used the passive protests method that had been practiced by Mohandas K. Gandhi in India in the protests against the British. He and other members of the clergy established the Southern Christian Leadership Conference (SCLC), and used non-violent measures such as boycotts, marches, and demonstrations to increase the awareness of how their civil rights were being denied. An example of such demonstrations was the 1960 sit-in where some African American college students took seats at the local 'white only' Woolworth's Cafeteria and refused to surrender them. They forced the cafeteria business to stop operating for an entire day. Martin Luther King encouraged the initiative and by the year 1961, there were over 70,000 individuals that took part in them. This was successful as it integrated public eating areas and helped desegregate other public facilities.

King, together with other SCLC members, went to extremes when they began protests in Birmingham, Alabama, which was known for its racism. King motivated teenagers and children to join in the movement as a way to increase its publicity. This led to his arrest and incarceration for eight days, but while in prison, he still wrote letters encouraging people to fight unjust laws. After his release, there were many protests and marches despite the efforts by police to intimidate the mob by making arrests. In 1963, John Kennedy sponsored more civil rights bills. NAACP activist Medgar Evers, a World War II veteran and college graduate, was assassinated the morning after a speech from the President. This led to the march on Washington DC in August of 1963 of over 250,000 people and Dr. King's famous "I Have a Dream" speech. In 1964, another Civil Rights Bill was passed, and Dr. King won the Nobel Peace Prize for his efforts.

In 1965, there were riots in Los Angeles, the Nation of Islam leader Malcolm X was assassinated, and there was violence against those that marched from Selma to Montgomery peacefully. It was during this time that a novel called *In the Heat of the Night* by John Ball was published. This book gave the story of an African American police officer Virgil Tibbs who was a victim of the mistreatment and indignity of racial discrimination. In December of that same year, Dr. Martin Luther King Jr. was appointed president of the Montgomery Improvement Association, directed the bus boycott, and became their spokesman. Meetings were held in his church to plan protest tactics and those meetings provided inspiration to all.

Pre-Workshop Activities

1. Talk to someone who was around during the civil rights movements of the 1950's and 1960's and ask them what they thought of Martin Luther King. Jr. and other activists.

2. Do you see any lingering signs of segregation and de facto discrimination?

Chapter 7: The Continuing Impact of Slavery and Racial Prejudice

Latisha was so proud! She was the first person in her family to walk across the stage as a college graduate. Her hard work and her mother's sacrifices had finally paid off. She already had a job in the city and was very excited about getting started on her career. But her joy and pride were diminished as she thought about her brother, murdered in a drug deal gone bad just a week ago. Her uncle was in prison, and she was afraid that it was just a matter of time before her cousin picked up a gun and tried to avenge her brother's death. She wondered how many more of the men in her family would get in trouble with the law. And she really wondered how she was going to keep her own sons in school and out of jail. She had to move away and she knew it, far away from the world she knew, just to keep her family safe.

It has been 170 years since the abolishment of slavery in the United States and seventy years since the civil rights movement in the 1950s and 1960s, but the negative consequences of racial prejudice and discrimination continue today. The legacy of slavery is seen every day in the challenges of African Americans.

After the Civil War, African Americans struggled to reconstruct their lives. White America's wealth and possessions were passed down from generation to generation, from fathers and grandfathers who owned lands, wealth, and money. Freed slaves almost always started from scratch, with no family wealth or even savings to help when times were tough.

Most of them had no formal schooling, either, which made them a largely illiterate community. They were deemed unworthy of the rights and privileges of white Americans by many people, and they were subject to a tremendous amount of stress that came from being seen as second-class citizens who were only provided with second-class opportunities.

This is the root of their economic status. The slaves were poor, had very few sources of income, and typically had no education. Life became even harder after slavery was abolished because they could no longer depend on their masters for basic needs. 170 years later, the African American community has continuing challenges with income levels, incarceration, education, mortality, and health issues. The disease of slavery is still sickening our society.

Income Levels

The chart below shows the state of American income last year based on race. Among the race groups, Asian households had the highest median income in 2023 ($112,800). The median income for non-Hispanic White households was $89,050, and it was $65,540 for Black households.

(source: https://www.census.gov/data/tables/time-series/demo/income-poverty/historical-income-households.html)

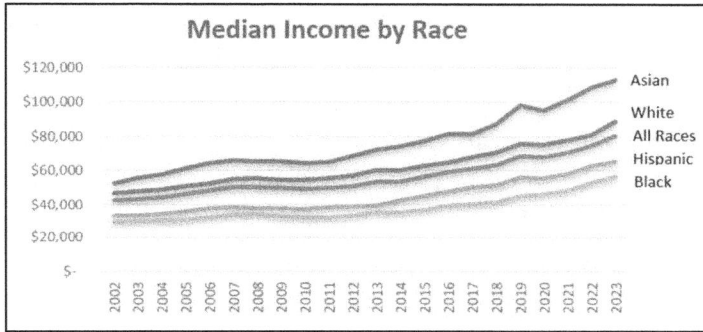

Median Income by Race

Legend: Asian, White, All Races, Hispanic, Black

(Y-axis: $120,000; $100,000; $80,000; $60,000; $40,000; $20,000; $-)
(X-axis years: 2002 through 2023)

Crime

According to the American Renaissance Foundation in their 2016 report on *The Color of Crime*, there are dramatic race differences in crime rates. Asians have the lowest rates, followed by whites, and then Hispanics. Blacks have notably high crime rates. This pattern holds true for virtually all crime categories and for virtually all age groups.

The evidence suggests that if there is a police racial bias in arrests, it is negligible. Victim and witness surveys show that police arrest violent criminals in close proportion to the rates at which criminals of different races commit violent crimes.

Both violent and non-violent crime has been declining in the United States since a high in 1993. 2015 saw a disturbing rise in murder in major American cities that some observers associated with "depolicing" in response to intense media and public scrutiny of police activity.

In 2013, a black was six times more likely than a non-black to commit murder, and 12 times more likely to murder someone of another race than to be murdered by someone of another race. In 2013, of the approximately 660,000 crimes of interracial violence that involved blacks and whites, blacks were the perpetrators 85 percent of the time. This meant a black person was 27 times more likely to attack a white person than vice versa. A Hispanic was eight times more likely to attack a white person than vice versa.

In 2014 in New York City, a black was 31 times more likely to be arrested for murder than a white, and a Hispanic was 12.4 times more likely. For the crime of "shooting" – defined as firing a bullet that hits someone – a black person was 98.4 times more likely than a white to be arrested, and a Hispanic was 23.6 times more likely.

In 2015, a black person was 2.45 times more likely than a white person to be shot and killed by the police. A Hispanic person was 1.21 times more likely. These figures are well within what would be expected given race differences in crime rates and the likelihood of resisting arrest.

In 2015, police killings of blacks accounted for approximately 4 percent of homicides of blacks. Police killings of unarmed blacks accounted for approximately 0.6 percent of homicides of blacks. The overwhelming majority of black homicide victims (93 percent from 1980 to 2008) were killed by blacks.

More recently, in 2019 Black people made up 12.2% of the U.S. population (U.S. Census Bureau, American Community Survey). Blacks, however, represent 26.6% of total arrests, including 51.2% of murder arrests, 52.7% of robbery arrests, 28.8% of burglary arrests, 28.6% of motor vehicle theft arrests, 42.2% of prostitution arrests, and 26.1% of drug arrests (FBI's Uniform Crime Report, Table 43).

Black residents also have the highest level of incarceration rates of any racial group. As of 2019, Blacks were incarcerated in local jails at a rate of 600 per 100,000 U.S. residents, which is more than three times the rate for Whites (184 per 100,000 U.S. residents) (Zeng and Minton 2021). The combined state and federal imprisonment rate for Black sentenced prisoners in 2019 was 1,096 per 100,000 U.S. residents compared to 214 per 100,000 U.S. residents for Whites (Carson 2020).

(source: https://oll.libertyfund.org/publications/liberty-matters/2024-02-13-systemic-racism-in-crime-do-blacks-commit-more-crimes-than-whites)

Incarceration

Another lasting impact of racial prejudice is the wrongful incarceration and excessive penalties that African Americans, American Indians, and Latinos suffer under the criminal justice system. Slavery itself was a form of incarceration, with families often being torn apart. So not only did freed slaves face economic disadvantages, but their family structures were also not stable. The African

American community was challenged with developing the social bonds and networks that are needed to maintain order.

Incarceration of blacks is five times more than that of whites; Hispanics are incarcerated almost twice as much as white people. Most African American families have at least one of their family members in prison. This reduces the human and financial resources in that homestead, making childbearing a struggle and contributing to children often developing unhealthy socialization behaviors.

Here's some recent statistics from the Bureau of Justice Statistics:

- As of the end of 2016, almost 2.5% of black male U.S. residents of all ages were imprisoned, as compared to 0.5% of white males. That is five times the rate.

- As of the end of 2016, about 34% of imprisoned males were black, 29% were white, and 24% were Hispanic. Among females in state or federal prison at the end of 2016, 46% were white, compared to 19% who were black and 18% who were Hispanic.

- The imprisonment rate for black females (97 per 100,000 black female residents) was almost double that for white females (49 per 100,000 white female residents).

- Black males had higher imprisonment rates across all age groups than all other races and Hispanic males.

- Black males ages 18 to 19 were 11.8 times more likely to be imprisoned than white males of the same age. This age group had the highest black-to-white racial disparity in 2016

- The difference between black and white female inmates of the same age was smaller, but still substantial. Black females ages 18 to 19 (33 inmates per 100,000) were almost 5 times more likely to be imprisoned than white females (7 inmates per 100,000). [See table on the following page]

Percent of sentenced prisoners under jurisdiction of state or federal correctional authorities, by sex, race, Hispanic origin, and age, December 31, 2016

Age group	Total[a]	Male					Female				
		All male[a]	White[b]	Black[b]	Hispanic	Other[b]	All female[a]	White[b]	Black[b]	Hispanic	Other[b]
Total[c]	100%	100%	100%	100%	100%	100%	100%	100%	100%	100%	100%
18–19	0.8	0.8	0.4	1.1	0.9	0.8	0.5	0.4	0.5	0.5	0.6
20–24	10.0	10.0	7.2	11.9	11.0	11.3	8.7	7.4	10.8	10.4	10.6
25–29	15.8	15.7	13.4	16.8	17.2	16.0	18.0	17.6	17.7	19.7	18.8
30–34	16.3	16.1	15.4	15.6	17.9	17.8	19.1	19.4	16.7	21.2	20.6
35–39	15.2	15.1	14.4	14.9	16.5	15.0	16.3	16.4	14.8	17.6	16.5
40–44	11.9	11.9	11.8	11.6	12.5	12.3	12.1	12.3	11.8	11.4	12.4
45–49	10.2	10.2	11.4	9.9	9.2	9.9	10.0	10.4	10.8	8.3	8.2
50–54	8.5	8.6	10.3	8.3	6.7	7.5	7.8	8.2	8.9	5.7	6.5
55–59	5.7	5.8	7.3	5.5	4.0	4.7	4.3	4.5	4.9	2.6	3.5
60–64	3.0	3.1	4.1	2.6	2.2	2.3	1.9	2.0	2.0	1.0	1.2
65 or older	2.6	2.7	4.3	1.7	1.8	2.3	1.3	1.6	1.0	1.0	1.2
Number of sentenced prisoners[d]	1,459,533	1,353,850	391,300	467,000	320,300	175,300	105,683	49,000	20,400	19,300	17,000

Note: Jurisdiction refers to the legal authority of state or federal correctional officials over a prisoner, regardless of where the prisoner is held. Counts are based on prisoners with sentences of more than 1 year under jurisdiction of state or federal correctional officials. Federal data include prisoners held in nonsecure, privately operated community corrections facilities and juveniles held in contract facilities. Includes imputed counts for North Dakota and Oregon, which did not submit 2016 NPS data. See Methodology.
[a]Includes American Indians and Alaska Natives; Asians, Native Hawaiians, and Other Pacific Islanders; and persons of two or more races.
[b]Excludes persons of Hispanic or Latino origin.
[c]Includes persons age 17 or younger.
[d]Rounded to the nearest 100.
Source: Bureau of Justice Statistics, National Prisoner Statistics (NPS), 2016; Federal Justice Statistics Program, 2016; National Corrections Reporting Program, 2015; and Survey of Prison Inmates, 2016 (preliminary).

Education Levels

Racial segregation in schools became a dominant feature of the American system of education after the end of slavery. African Americans who were privileged to attend school did not often have the opportunity to choose the best schools. There were private schools for the white and public schools for the black in the South. However, most African Americans did not get an opportunity to go to school. Their schools received fewer funds and had a huge number of students. The infrastructure was typically poor, and the quality of certified teachers was lower compared to white districts.

According to Wikipedia, while the educational attainment of all races increased during the 1990s, with the gap between African Americans and non-Hispanic whites decreasing, differences between the races remain, especially among those with a bachelor's degree or higher. Asian Americans had the highest educational attainment of any race, followed by whites who had a higher percentage of high school graduates but a lower percentage of college graduates. Persons identifying as Hispanic or Latino, without regard to race, had the lowest educational attainment. The gap was the largest between foreign-born Asian Americans, over half (50.1%) of whom had a bachelor's degree or higher and foreign-born Hispanics, only 9.8% of whom had a four-year college degree.

Hispanics and Latinos also trailed far behind in terms of graduating from high school; it was the only major group for which high school graduates constituted less than 80%

of the population. This large inequality might partially be explained through the influx of uneducated foreign-born Hispanic Americans who had not been offered the chance to complete secondary education in their home country and who had not completed secondary education in the United States.

Overall, nearly half (49.8%) of Asian Americans, nearly a third (30%) of non-Hispanic Whites, 17.3% of non-Hispanic Blacks, and just over a tenth (11.4%) of Hispanics or Latinos had a four-year college degree. The same differences decrease significantly at the high school level with 89.4% of non-Hispanic whites, 87.6% of Asian Americans, 80.0% of African Americans, and 57% of Hispanics or Latinos having graduated from high school.[2]

The Racial achievement gap in the United States refers to these educational disparities between minority students and Caucasian students. Evidence of the racial achievement gap remains present today because not all groups of students are advancing at the same rates. The racial achievement gap has many individual and economic implications and there have been many efforts in education reform to narrow this gap.

(HigherEducation.org reports similar statistics.)

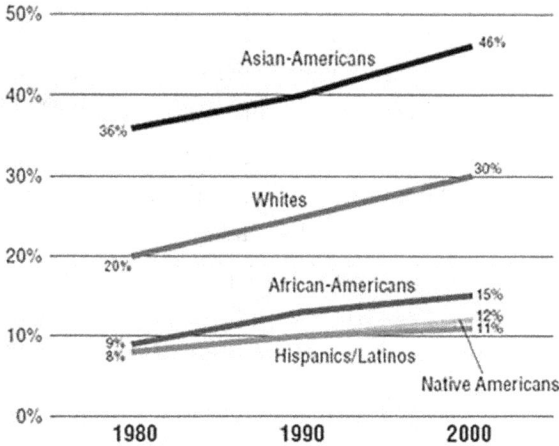

Figure 5. The percentage of the working-age population (ages 25 to 64) with a bachelor's degree or higher has increased for all racial/ethnic groups, but the gaps between groups have widened.

Notes: Pacific Islanders are included with Asian-Americans. Alaska Natives are included with Native Americans.
Source: U.S. Census Bureau, 5% Public Use Microdata Samples (based on 1980, 1990, and 2000 Census).

Mortality Rates and General Well-Being

Slavery and racial prejudice have also affected the mortality rates of minority groups in America. After the abolishment of slavery, most African Americans struggled to survive, and many died. Segregated communities are still exposed to crimes and violence more often because of the poverty levels. Their neighborhoods are simply not as safe as white communities. Acts of violence lead to the death of adults and children and increase the mortality rate among African Americans. Shootings in the black neighborhoods have been on the rise with the perception that such crimes are associated with black people. Lack of better health care systems is another contributing factor the higher mortality levels. Very few can afford to pay hospital bills and get necessary medications.

Low-income communities, regardless of racial composition, experience health problems as well. Most of their neighborhoods are exposed to environmental hazards. They do not have proper housing facilities. The houses are mostly crowded, lack temperature and humidity regulators, have elevated noise levels and are more exposed to allergens such as mold and dust and lead paints. With such living conditions, there are higher chances of contracting diseases such as asthma and sleeplessness. Black and Latino neighborhoods also have fewer parks where children can play. Recreational centers and swimming pools are rare. Most children are not allowed to play outside because it is not safe, and mostly spend their time in the house playing video games, watching TV, and eating. These are some of the contributing factors to obesity, diabetes, and cardiovascular diseases in minority groups. Without much physical activity in a child's life, as an adult, they are more likely to have health problems.

Family Issues

Child Trends reports that the percent of births to unmarried women has been steadily increasing from 1990 to 2016. The most recent report is for 2016 shows:

Racial or ethnic group	Percent of births considered "non marital"
Non-Hispanic whites	28%
Hispanics	52%
Non-Hispanic blacks	69%

(https://www.childtrends.org/publications/dramatic-increase-in-percentage-of-births-outside-marriage-among-whites-hispanics-and-women-with-higher-education-levels)

In 2013, CNN anchor Don Lemon gave an on-air commentary that went viral on social media. The No. 1 item on his list of problems on which the black community should focus "and probably the most important," he said -- had to do with out-of-wedlock births. "Just because you can have a baby, it doesn't mean you should," Lemon said. "Especially without planning for one or getting married first. More than 72 percent of children in the African American community are born out of wedlock. That means absent fathers. And the studies show that lack of a male role model is an express train right to prison and the cycle continues."

Children in Single-Parent Families by Race
Data Provided by KIDS COUNT

Location	Race	Data Type	2012	2013	2014	2015	2016
United States	American Indian	Number	345,000	329,000	341,000	333,000	339,000
		Percent	53%	52%	53%	52%	52%
	Asian and Pacific Islander	Number	579,000	557,000	578,000	568,000	572,000
		Percent	17%	16%	17%	16%	16%
	Black or African American	Number	6,493,000	6,427,000	6,382,000	6,333,000	6,281,000
		Percent	67%	67%	66%	66%	66%
	Hispanic or Latino	Number	7,008,000	7,044,000	7,190,000	7,180,000	7,230,000
		Percent	42%	42%	42%	42%	42%
	Non-Hispanic White	Number	9,358,000	9,289,000	9,181,000	8,998,000	8,766,000
		Percent	25%	25%	25%	25%	24%
	Two or more races	Number	1,703,000	1,758,000	1,797,000	1,804,000	1,900,000
		Percent	43%	43%	42%	41%	42%
	Total	Number	24,725,000	24,647,000	24,689,000	24,444,000	24,267,000
		Percent	35%	35%	35%	35%	35%

Pre-Workshop Activities

1. What continuing impact of racial discrimination to you see today, or with which you have firsthand experience?

2. Do you know anyone, or have any family members in prison? How about in poverty? What does that feel like to them and their families?

Chapter 8: It's Not Just Black and White

Jose was confused. He had lived in California all of his life, and now he and his family were being deported to Mexico. They had to give up their home, their business, and all of their friends. His father was encouraged to come to America during the Second World War and was now being told he had to leave! It just wasn't fair. He thought to himself: "Now I know how the black slaves must have felt", as he and his family were loaded into a truck, to be sent to a land he had never known.

While we have been focusing on challenges of black Americans, racial prejudice and discrimination is hardly just a black and white issue. As it turns out, our European ancestors also created a culture of discrimination that affected many racial communities.

It started when the European settlers first came to the American continent. While friendly at first, they soon began to push Native Americans from their homeland, essentially stealing their homes and driving them into near-oblivion. Natives were seen as inferior; they were used and then abused, and in many ways, still are today.

In the early 1800's, after England and other nations had banned slavery, it became increasingly difficult to buy new slaves. So the white majority invited workers from other nations to come to America to provide much needed labor. They encouraged immigration with the promise of employment, but within a few decades turned on those whom they had encouraged to come and work for them. In some cases, they even deported them after they had served their purpose.

Chinese Discrimination

Beginning in the 1850's with the gold rush, Chinese workers came to America to work not just in the mines, but also in building railroads, in factories, and in the textile industry. Many of them wanted to become entrepreneurs, too, which greatly disturbed the white majority. After the projects for which they initially came to the US were completed, they were willing to work harder for less money, so they also threatened the jobs of non-Chinese workers.

As a result, Chinese immigrants were widely disparaged. The Yellow Peril movement was born in the late 1800's, essentially saying that the Western world was in great danger from Asian countries. There was much racist literature and condemnation of Asian cultures as inferior, drug addicted, of lower morale character, and a threat to white racial purity.

States passed legislation to restrict the number of Chinese immigrants and make it difficult for them to vote and get business licenses. While this legislation was generally overturned in federal courts, the anti-Chinese sentiment and the intentions were very clear. In 1882, Congress passed the Chinese Exclusion Act, which put a stop to Chinese immigration for 10 years. It was later expanded to include Hawaii and the Philippines, and was eventually extended indefinitely. The act was repealed in 1943 to improve the relations with China, who was an important wartime ally at the time.

Japanese Discrimination

Japanese immigrants, while not arriving in the great numbers of the Chinese immigrants, were also held in low regard and targeted after the Chinese Exclusion Act of 1882. California was especially harsh, and passed legislation to prevent Japanese citizens from owning land to reduce farming competition with the white landowners.

The discrimination and prejudice were greatly increased in World War II. After Japan attacked Pearl Harbor, anyone of Japanese descent was discriminated against. 110,000 of them ended up in "War Relocation Camps", and many had their land confiscated under the guise that they were a threat to national security.

After World War II, many in power had terrible memories of the Japanese, and the prejudice continued. The tag of "made in Japan" was seen to be a confession of poor quality, and it wasn't until Japan became a powerhouse in electronics and automobiles in the 1970's and 1980's that the general opinion of the Japanese culture turned around.

Irish Discrimination

Many in the US despised the Irish, too. This was left over from England's anti-Irish sentiment, but also sprang from a mass immigration of Irish countrymen during and after the great potato famine from 1845 to 1852. Over two million Irish immigrated to the US, and like other tribes, were willing to work for lower wages. They talked funny, had unusual customs, and were mostly Catholic, which also caused them to be disparaged by the white majority.

Hispanic Discrimination

Spain invaded Mexico in 1519, conquered the Aztec empire, and in just two short years declared victory. They began colonizing, and eventually took over the country, popularizing the Spanish language and the Catholic Faith.

Mexicans began establishing Catholic missions in what is now the Southwestern part of the US beginning in 1769. After Mexico won its independence from Spain in 1821, the missions were taken over by the new government and used as bases for expansion. They forced natives into settlements and stole their land much in the same way that English settlers did to other Native Americans on the East Coast. Large cities, including Los Angeles, San Diego, San Jose, and San Francisco, sprung up from these missions.

Mexico also expanded into what is now Texas and New Mexico. But the Texans rebelled and fought back in the Texas Revolution. The famous battle of the Alamo in San Antonio in 1836 was an important part of the Revolution and has been the subject of many books and movies that demonized Mexicans as an evil enemy. The Mexican-American war of 1846-1848 and the Spanish American war of 1898 further created a harsh edge to Mexican American relations.

But, as with the Chinese before, Mexicans were seen as a source of cheap labor. Many "temporary" Mexican workers were encouraged and permitted in World War I, but thereafter, the Border Patrol was established and immigration was strongly discouraged. In 1932 there were mass deportations.

In World War II, Mexicans were again seen as a source of cheap labor to make up for the lack of factory and farm workers caused by so many young white men fighting in the war. And as before, when the war ended there was a mass deportation, this time 3.8 million people were deported to Mexico from 1954 to 1958, with Operation Wetback.

Other Discrimination in the US

The white protestant majority in the US didn't just discriminate against Blacks, Chinese, Japanese, and Hispanics, they seem to discriminate, often with great cruelty, against any population that didn't look like them, talk like them, and worship at the same altars.

Over the history of the US, that discrimination has been leveled at the LGBTQ community, the homeless, obese people, women, Catholics, and Jews. And despite the laws requiring fair and equal treatment, regardless of race, color, creed, age, or sexual orientation, that discrimination continues today.

It's Not Just an American Problem

While this book focuses on the issues of black people in the USA, that is far from the only occurrence of racism in the world today. We humans see things superficially and rush to judgement. **People are guilty of an "us and them" mentality all over the world.**

In India, lower "classes" are discriminated against by higher castes. In Indonesia, Chinese students are not given educational opportunities.

In Japan, "Hafus", or those of mixed racial heritage are often called terrible names. People with dual citizenship must choose only one country when they are 22. Japan doesn't have a lot of diversity, so those of a different heritage stand out and are often ostracized.

In Australia, the Aborigines were discriminated against for centuries, and as recently as 25 years ago, a major political party had a platform of refusing immigration to non-whites. As in the US, Muslims are also judged to be less trustworthy and of a lower class.

And it was only a few decades ago that Apartheid in South Africa legally segregated the African population from the Europeans.

So the problem is not just black and white, and it isn't just in the US. Once we make progress on issues in the US, we can help others around the world solve their problems, too.

Pre-Workshop Activities

1. What discrimination have you seen towards tribes other than blacks? Do you ever hear people putting down Hispanics, Jews, Middle Eastern people, or Asian Americans?

2. Do you have any friends or family members who are of Asian or Mexican descent? How do you feel about discrimination towards them?

3. Ask your colleagues and friends who have recently been to or arrived from other countries about racism in their home countries.

4. Spend a few minutes looking up racial tensions in one or two foreign countries.

Chapter 9: The Solution to Racism

Fortunately for us, there is a solution. What you can do largely depends on whether you are black or white, Hispanic or Asian, and your age and economic status, but there are many things you can do no matter who you are.

First, understand that we can and must overcome our prejudices. In this cosmopolitan, high-technology world, our species must heal from this disease; we must evolve or die. If we persist in our tribal warfare, pack hunting, "us and them" heritage, we will surely suffer greatly as our world grows smaller and weapon technologies become more deadly. **To be clear, our tribal instinct and predisposition to see the world in terms of "us and them", where "them" is often the enemy, is the biggest threat to the survival of the human species.**

Second, understand the source of our prejudice. Understand that prejudice is a social disease, passed from generation to generation. We catch it from our mothers and fathers, our preachers and teachers, and from other powerful and strong people who blame members of other tribes for their own problems in an effort to feel better about themselves. It is far easier to blame "them" than it is to take personal responsibility. Our subconscious minds are always on the lookout for danger, and those who do not look, act, talk, and think like us are perceived to be dangerous.

Third, have a new attitude towards the challenges of the black community. If you are white, accept that your ancestors most likely benefited from the kidnapping and imprisonment of millions of innocent people. Some of your ancestors may have been directly involved; they may have even been slave owners or worse. That is your legacy. You have a responsibility to clean up your ancestors' mess.

If you are a black American, recognize that while there are still many who perpetuate the ignorance and cruelty of past generations, there are many who do not and are working to help you overcome your challenges. But you must take personal responsibility for your actions and attitudes. You have to believe in yourself and do the work necessary to build a strong and healthy life for yourself and your family. Many people, including Oprah Winfrey, Barrack Obama, and many famous athletes and celebrities will show you the way.

Fourth, focus on eliminating the tactics of prejudice. Start by taking personal responsibility. Catch and stop yourself from expressing prejudicial thoughts and feelings. By all means, don't use dehumanizing terms when referring to members of other tribes. And then call out those around you when they express prejudicial thoughts and feelings. Recognize and express disapproval with prejudice when it happens around you. Speak up when others express prejudicial thoughts and use dehumanizing terms, even when they are an authority – I would say *especially* when they are an authority. If your preachers, teachers, priests, and business leaders use dehumanizing terms and express prejudicial thoughts against members of different tribes, speak up against that. If your mothers, fathers, brothers, sisters, and friends start down the road of blaming and shaming others because of the color of their skin or the way they talk, just tell them you aren't going there.

When you see friends promoting videos that paint other tribes in a bad light, with the intentional or unintentional side effect of generalizing the negative behavior to the entire race, just say "no". Speak up and say something like "of course you know that not all whites / blacks / Asians / Christians / Muslims / Jews / Democrats / Republicans act that way."

In your community, we urge you to organize or sponsor workshops on Curing Racism for community leaders, public officials, businesses, PTAs, teachers, and/or children.

Do your part, too. Go out of your way to make friends with those of different races and get your families to interact. Get to know them as people – ask them about their lives, their loves, their families, and their dreams. Get to know their hearts.

When you are in a group, don't allow it to divide into races. Walk across the aisle and sit down with other tribes. Be friendly. Be open. Connect.

Above all, play with and interact with the children. You will see the similarities in them. You will learn to see the greatness in everyone. And then you, too, will part of the solution.

Chapter 10: The Not-too-Distant Future

As she looked over her family, Makir couldn't help but smile. There were so many cultures, so many faces. Her eldest had married a light-skinned gentleman, and the others took great pride in finding spouses from other cultures, too. The grandchildren were all mixed — every one of them — and she could not possibly love them more.

She remembered a time not too long ago, when, as a child, she had been down and out and frowned upon just because she looked different. It was even illegal to date or, God-forbid, marry a person of another race. But now the world had become wiser, more loving, and more accepting. It had even become a badge of honor of sorts to have a diverse family.

And somehow, her melting pot of a family had allowed her and all of its members — not to mention everyone who knew them all — to see beyond the superficial. They looked each other in the eye. They saw each other's hearts. They listened with the intention of understanding and supporting each other.

And they loved one another — deeply, profoundly, and unconditionally.

There will come a time in the not-too-distant future when it will be rare thing for a family not to have some mixtures of cultures and skin colors. Our world is shrinking and becoming more cosmopolitan. We are exposed to other tribes and cultures far more than we were just a few decades ago. And with the interaction comes the understanding, the compassion, and the love.

It's a future that is coming, no doubt about it. Let's do everything we can to hurry it along.

Chapter 11: Summary and Next Steps

In summary:

- There is only one race: the human race. The differences we see are cultural and due to evolution in isolation.

- We need families and tribes to survive. Tribalism is a subconscious, inherited survival strategy, fine-tuned through eons of evolution.

- Tribal warfare was a natural part of the evolution of the species, as tribes battled for survival over limited resources, and then fought to maintain power. Tribal conflict is the underlying cause of all our wars and is the biggest threat to the survival of mankind.

- Racism is a form of tribalism and placism, but it is far from the only one.

- Those who are prejudicial and discriminatory are caught up in their "us and them" mentality, blame "them" for their own struggles, and put "them" down so that they can feel more powerful and safer themselves.

- While racial prejudice is natural result of our tribal and warring nature, it is mostly learned and can be overcome.

- While it is difficult to do, we can and must reject the prejudicial attitudes held by our peers and by those in leadership positions. We must learn to police our own tribes. Speaking out when we notice others being prejudicial and discriminatory is essential.

- The terrible impact of slavery continues today, and we have a lot of work to do to heal the wounds caused by our ancestors. Making the black community stronger, one person at a time, makes all of us stronger.

- The issue isn't just black and white. The white protestant majority in the US has a history of racial prejudice and discrimination against other tribes, too.

- Getting to know people personally who don't look like us, talk like us, or dress like us is the critical first step. We have to spend time with them and get to know them as well as we know members of our own families and tribes. As we say, racism is overcome "One Conversation, Once Connection, One Heart at a Time."

- When we overcome our personal prejudices, we can begin to help others overcome theirs, too.

- When we learn to see through the superficial differences that divide us, we will be able to discover the common values that unite us.

- Hold a baby from another tribe in your arms. Get to know the children. Talk with them. Play with them. Love them as if they were your own. Because in a very real sense, they are.

About the Authors

Paul Hoyt

Paul Hoyt has been working to be the best person he can be for well over 60 years. He is the creator of Mind Sequencing, a revolutionary approach to personal development and stress relief, and the founder of The Focused Mind Community and The GoodPower Project.

A business consultant and fractional CFO for 24 years, he brings his passion for organization and facts to the world of personal development.

This is his seventh inspirational work. He published *Remember - A Simple and Gentle Pathway to Spirit* in 2005, and *The Practice of Awakening – 150 Ways to Raise Your Consciousness Whenever You Choose* in 2010. He is the best-selling author of *The Practice of Awakening II – The First Light of Joy* (2013). Other works include *The Levels of Creation* (2016), *Surprises on the Road to Enlightenment* (2023), and *Determining Truth* (2024)

You can learn more about him and his teachings at
www.GoodPowerProject.com,
www.MindSequencing.com,
www.TheFocusedMindCommunity.com, and
www.PaulHoyt.com.

Pas Simpson

Pas Simpson, aka "The Happiness Engineer" and "Mr. I Love My Life!" spreads joy from his very first smile. Whether in his daily videos, lighting up a stage or in his coaching sessions, Pas' mission to help create a happier, healthier, wealthier world is evident. He teaches people how to make the choice of happiness and to define what success personally feels like to them.

Pas has dedicated his business and life to opening doors that were previously closed for others. It became a natural transition when deciding to get involved with his local community, especially when it comes to helping gang members and returning citizens deal with the violence that has shaped their narrative.

Pas has been dedicated to fighting the disease of violence. Poverty is violence and most other acts of violence are results of being impoverished. He works with returning citizens and those easily forgotten, helping them find success with "the four E's": Education, Entrepreneurship, Employment, and Emotional Support. Pas has realized that opportunity is the antidote to violence and uses his smile to share that message wherever he goes.

You can find out more about Pas at www.JoyfulFunds.com and www.MyHappinessEngineer.com.